MOON
SHOWER

Text copyright © 2023 by Jane Yolen and Ryan G. Van Cleave
Illustration copyright © 2023 by Luis San Vicente

Published by Moonshower, an imprint of Bushel & Peck Books.
All rights reserved. No part of this publication may be reproduced
without written permission from the publisher.

Bushel & Peck Books is a family-run publishing house based in Fresno, California, that
believes in uplifting children with the highest standards of art, music, literature, and
ideas. Find beautiful books for gifted young minds at www.bushelandpeckbooks.com.

Our family is dedicated to fighting illiteracy all over the world. For every book we sell,
we donate one to a child in need—book for book. To nominate a school or organization to
receive free books, please visit www.bushelandpeckbooks.com.

Type set in Aunt Mildred and Circus Sideshow.
Icons and speech bubble shapes licensed from Shutterstock.com

LCCN: 2023935121
ISBN: 978-1-63819-201-5

First Edition

Printed in China

1 3 5 7 9 10 8 6 4 2

BODY MUSIC

POEMS ABOUT THE NOISES YOUR BODY MAKES

JANE YOLEN &
RYAN G. VAN CLEAVE

Illustrated by
LUIS SAN VICENTE

BODY MUSIC

My tummy rumbles,
my knees go pop.
Are my toes cracking
as I skip and hop?

I sniffle, I snort.
I laugh, I snore.
One time my belch
opened a door!

My neck? It creaks.
My nose? It whistles.
My butt makes a BOOM
like exploding missiles!

I'm a walking chorus—
this is my shtick.
Sit back and enjoy
my body music!

—RVC

 WHAT IS BODY MUSIC?

It can be accidental sounds, or responses to pain, surprise, and fear. But there are also folk traditions of many different countries that use body percussion, which is the art of using parts of the body to create vibrations and sounds.

DID YOU KNOW?

Examples of body percussion include West Africa's hambone, Ethiopian armpit music, hand clapping in Spanish flamenco, Inuit throat singing, and Maori haka.

? WHAT IS A FART?

Gas in your belly builds up when you eat and at the same time swallow air. Small amounts travel through your body along the digestive track. More gas is made as the food breaks down. And suddenly you have a stomach full of gas. It has to go somewhere. It goes down and out. And that's a fart! Sometimes loud, sometimes with no sound at all. And sometimes with an awful smell.

DOUBLE WHAMMY

Cough heads north,
fart goes south.
One by bottom,
the other by mouth.

Only bad when they
blow together.
Enough to bring a house down,
or move a feather.

I heard of a man
who did both on stage.
In Paris, doncha know,
he was quite the rage.

So, why does Mom always
get so upset?
I haven't brought the house down.
At least not yet.

—JY

DID YOU KNOW?

In France during the late nineteenth/early twentieth century, a baker called Le Pétomane performed farts on the Paris stage as a "fartiste." He could fart songs like the French national anthem and make sounds like thunderstorms and cannons firing.

UNINVITED GUEST

Hiccups erupt at the worst of times,
Like when eating noodles or counting dimes.
Big brother laughs. Little sister cries.
My hiccups echo into the skies!

I hold my breath. I chug lemon juice.
These horrible hiccups just won't vamoose!
I lick honey. I sip vinegar.
Yet I HIC!! myself right off furniture.

I breathe in a bag. I drink upside down.
I'm a HIC! machine from Hiccup Town.
Scaring doesn't work. And peanut butter? Nope.
I've even considered munching on soap!

I can't watch TV. I can't nosh chips.
I can't believe the noise coming from my lips.
At least my hiccups aren't contagious—
a roomful of them would be outrageous.

Uh oh!

Hic.

HIC.

HIC!

—RVC

? WHAT IS A HICCUP?

A hiccup is the involuntary spasm of the muscles around the lungs. Air rushes into your throat so fast that the vocal cords close for a moment, creating the distinctive noise that we call hiccups. Most hiccups are caused by eating or drinking too quickly.

💡 DID YOU KNOW?

Charles Osborne, an Iowa farmer, hiccupped for 68 years straight!

THAT
SUDDEN
GROANER

You groan,
you moan.
A tear drips
from your eye.

You ache,
you make
another groaning
cry.

It seems quite odd
the body acts
this way.

Cause soon
it's gone,
and you get up
to play.

—JY

 WHAT IS A GROAN?

It has been called "a deep, inarticulate sound" that quite often signifies pain but can also mean pleasure (for a bad pun, a rich piece of chocolate cake, a lovely song, or an adorable baby).

 DID YOU KNOW?

Humans and animals are not the only groaners. Water pipes sometimes groan, as do toilets and showers (which are connected to water pipes).

SNAP, CRACKLE, POP!

I SNAP

        like the cap of my favorite root beer bottle.

I CRACKLE

        like a bag of microwave popcorn.

I POP

        like a bubble of overblown gum.

I LOVE

        to make a fingertastic ruckus.

I WISH

        more people enjoyed the music within us.

—RVC

? WHAT IS A KNUCKLE CRACK?

No one knows for sure why knuckles "crack," but many people believe that moving/stretching a joint creates a small air pocket that arrives with a SNAP, CRACKLE, or POP! Others say the movement of ligaments around a joint causes that sharp popping sound.

DID YOU KNOW?

20% of people regularly crack their knuckles. Are you a frequent snap, crackle, and pop-er?

WHAT IS A SNEEZE?

A sneeze is the sudden—and often violent—expulsion of air from the nose and mouth. Your sneeze reflex happens when something irritates the passages of your nose and stimulates the nerves there.

DID YOU KNOW?

The expelled air from a sneeze can reach 40 mph or more!

 ## WHAT IS A WHEEZE?

A wheeze is a strained whistling sound that happens when you breathe. It's generally caused by an inflammation in the throat or lungs, or an airway that's narrowed by an allergic reaction or a foreign object that's been inhaled. Many of the causes for wheezing are serious, so take appropriate medicine or visit a doctor if needed!

DID YOU KNOW?

Animals wheeze, too. This includes snakes, which often wheeze or make clicking noises when they're almost ready to shed their skin.

GESUNDHEIT!

I don't know what's worse—
the sneeze or the wheeze.
One's jet, wet and noisy,
the other's pure squeeze.

My allergies can strike
any time, any place.
So, don't cut the grass,
or dust that bookcase.

Please skip the roses,
And adiós the new cat.
Wipe off kitchen shelving,
and wash the bathmat.

Hold on a moment . . .
I feel something brewing.
A sneeze? A wheeze?
I'm unsure what is stewing.

Ah . . .

AH . . .

CHOO!

I'm through!

—RVC

THAT OLD KNOTTY SNOTTY QUESTION

What is the difference
twixt sniffle and snuffle?
One is a toadstool,
the other a truffle.

One is more elegant,
almost polite.
The other is lower class,
out for a fight.

Both try controlling
a drizzle of snot.
One is quite loud,
but the other is not.

One you can catch with
a cloth, I believe.
The other you swipe
with the edge of your sleeve.

Snuffle or sniffle,
it's quite up to you.
But if my node was rudning,
I'd know what I'd do.

—JY

? WHAT ARE SNIFFLES AND SNUFFLES?

Both are conditions of a head cold with a runny nose. It's almost automatic to try and breathe up the trickle that wants to drop down. Both words mean "breathe in quickly and repeatedly through the nose."

DID YOU KNOW?

Rabbits can develop a bad case of snuffles that is very dangerous to them, unlike humans who just find it annoying.

A FAST CATCH
OF BREATH

Three things make me gasp.
One of them—an asp.*
Another one is heights.
The third—airplane flights.

*An asp's a kind of snake.
 Any kind makes me quake.

—JY

WHAT IS A GASP?

It's a short, quick intake of breath through the mouth, usually because of surprise, pain, or sometimes, a shock.

DID YOU KNOW?

The term "last gasp" refers to the last breath a person takes before death.

A SLEEPY POEM

My yawn

    goes on

        and on

            and on

            like an

        endless

    slooooow

tired song.

Won't
you
play
along?

—RVC

WHAT IS A YAWN?

A yawn is a reflexive action where your mouth opens wide and you inhale deeply. Scientists aren't exactly sure what a yawn's health benefits are, though being bored or tired are two common causes for a yaaaaaaawn.

DID YOU KNOW?

Yawning seems to be contagious. Try yawning in front of a family member and see what happens. (It sometimes even works when you yawn at a dog or cat!)

A PULSE
(for Peter)

It's the body's
constant beat.
The music running
head to feet.
Composers use
compulsively
the pulse's beeps
instinctually.
And if that beeping
pulse is gone?

Well . . .
you won't be here
very long!

—JY

? WHAT IS A PULSE?

A pulse is the rhythmic
movement of blood
through a body. It's most
easily felt in the wrists or
neck because blood vessels
are closer to the skin there.

💡 DID YOU KNOW?

Many things can raise
your pulse rate, such as
standing, feeling anxious,
or even being in hot
weather.

FINGER SNAP

With a click,
with a crack,
with a shake
and a snap,

I can call you
to attention,
you can signal me back.

It's a shock,
it's a pause,
it's a cool dude's
applause.

We make
body music
clickily
just
because.

—JY

? WHAT IS A FINGER SNAP?

A finger snap happens when a finger is pressed
against the thumb and brought down quickly
against the palm of a hand. Sometimes people
use finger snaps as a substitute for clapping.

💡 DID YOU KNOW?

The finger snap is fast! It's more than 20 times
faster than an eyeblink.

THAT GIGGLE

That giggle
makes me wiggle.
It's a tickle
in my throat.

It makes some people
laugh out loud,
and makes some others
gloat.

—JY

? **WHAT IS A GIGGLE?**

WHAT IS A GIGGLE?

Giggles are silly bursts of laughter that usually come from someone being amused or embarrassed. People are said to have "the giggles" when they can't stop laughing.

 DID YOU KNOW?

People laugh and giggle 30 times more often when they are around other people.

SNORE

It's hard to ignore
my daddy's big snore.
Why, it shakes every part
of the house.

It's been known to destroy
my favorite toy,
and kill a poor
innocent mouse.

It's a tumble of rumbles,
that sounds like close thunder.
It makes both dogs go under
the bed!

The only one sleeping
is Pa, and he's keeping
the rest of us all
seeing red.

—JY

WHAT IS A SNORE?

A snore is breathing
with snorting or
grunting noises while
asleep. It happens
because the muscles
relax in the mouth,
throat, and nose,
interfering with the
flow of air.

DID YOU KNOW?

Only about 60% of
snorers are aware that
they snore.

STOMACH SONG

What's that bubbly rumbling?
That loud and gurgly grumbling?

That brassy gassy something—
it's so much more than mumbling!

That echoey growl is bumbling,
crumbling, rumbling, stumbling.

Oops!
This is humbling.

The thunderous noise a-tumbling
is
coming
out
of
me . . .
It's troubling!

—RVC

 WHAT IS A TUMMY GROWL?

Digestion is a noisy process already, but it can get even louder when you eat spicy foods, swallow a lot of air, or have some fizzy drinks.

DID YOU KNOW?

The acid produced by stomachs to digest food is strong enough to dissolve most metals.

BODY PERCUSSION

The body, the body,
a wonderful thing.
It can sound like a drum.
It can rumble and ring!
It can shudder and mutter,
and sometimes can sing.
A thin skin of music
tied up by blood string.

The body, the body,
an instrument fine.
It can sneeze, it can whistle,
wheeze, whisper, and whine.
It can cough, oft that's needed,
and fart out of line.
A skin bag of sounds
tied with hairy twine.

—JY

 WHAT IS BODY PERCUSSION?

Body percussion is simply a type of body music. It's like a dance party for your body, where you're the DJ and the instruments at the same time!

DID YOU KNOW?

Orchestras have an entire section called "percussion," but not because the players are laughing, groaning, farting, or coughing. It's because their instruments—drums, cymbals, triangles, and other such instruments—make loud sounds/noise when pounded or slammed together. Can you think of other percussion instruments?

ABOUT JANE YOLEN

Jane Yolen comes from a family of writers and snorers. Her mother and father wrote adult books and short stories. They both snored. Her brother works today as a journalist. He snores, too. Her three children each have well over thirty books published, and two of her six grandchildren have one and two books to their credit. And EVERYONE in the family snores. LOUDLY. Jane, herself, has published over 400 books (*Body Music* is probably the 419th!). She lives in Hatfield, MA. Visit janeyolen.com, @Jane.Yolen on Facebook, @JaneYolen on Twitter, and @JYolen on Instagram.

ABOUT RYAN G. VAN CLEAVE

Ryan G. Van Cleave wrote his first poem at age five, and he's been writing, reading, and loving poetry ever since. As the Picture Book Whisperer, he helps celebrities and high-profile clients write picture books and kidlit projects. Ryan once belched loud enough to startle a dog out of an afternoon nap from three rooms over. Visit Ryan at www.ryangvancleave.com or www.thepicturebookwhisperer.com.

ABOUT LUIS SAN VICENTE

The works of Mexico City artist Luis San Vicente have been exhibited in Mexico, Venezuela, Europe, and the U.S. He has won UNESCO's prestigious NOMA Encouragement Concours Prize for Illustration, and UNESCO honored his work (1997, 1998, and 1999) in their prestigious Youth and Children's Catalog of Illustrations.

MOON
SHOWER

ABOUT MOONSHOWER

Moonshower is the poetry imprint of Bushel & Peck Books. It publishes beautiful, illustrated volumes of poetry for kids of all ages by some of the world's leading poets.

BUSHEL
& PECK
BOOKS

ABOUT BUSHEL & PECK BOOKS

Bushel & Peck Books is a children's publishing house with a special mission. Through our Book-for-Book Promise™, we donate one book to kids in need for every book we sell. Our beautiful books are given to kids through schools, libraries, local neighborhoods, shelters, nonprofits, and also to many selfless organizations who are working hard to make a difference. So thank you for purchasing this book! Because of you, another book will find its way into the hands of a child who needs it most.